S.O.S

SINK OR SWIM: GINGER TOES!

WRITTEN BY NIEVES CATAHAN VILLAMIN
ILLUSTRATED BY
PAUL LUCERO & PAULINE LUCERO

This publication contains the opinions and ideas of its author. It is intended to provide helpful and informative material on the subjects addressed in the publication. The author and publisher specifically disclaim all responsibility for any liability, loss or risk, personal or otherwise, which is incurred as a consequence, directly or indirectly, of the use and application of any of the contents of this book.

WORKBOOK PRESS LLC
187 E Warm Springs Rd,
Suite B285, Las Vegas, NV 89119, USA

Website:	https://workbookpress.com/
Hotline:	1-888-818-4856
Email:	admin@workbookpress.com

Ordering Information:
Quantity sales. Special discounts are available on quantity purchases by corporations, associations, and others. For details, contact the publisher at the address above.

Library of Congress Control Number:
ISBN-13:   000-0-00000-000-0 (Paperback Version)
                   000-0-00000-000-0 (Digital Version)

REV. DATE: 09/20/2022

THE BAMBOO TREE

A very long time ago, in a far, faraway land, there lived a king who was loved and respected by the people he ruled because he was kind and compassionate. The laws he handed down were all fair and just, such that the villagers obeyed without asking any questions. He served with love and compassion, so his constituents loved him even more. The people desired to keep him in power for generations.

Many years later, a new heir ascended the throne with a different style of rule. The progeny named Rajah Kawayan ruled the kingdom by force. He was unkind and heartless. He showed no respect for anyone. He brutally punished those who violated his orders.

One day, a vagabond walked into the palace and begged the king for food. He was starved and famished, having had no food for many days. The king roared and threw him out of the palace.

"You're lazy. Shame on you for not wanting to work! All you ever do is beg and beg and beg. Don't ever show your face to me again, or I will feed you to my lions and tigers!"

But the beggar shouted in an equally loud voice, "I pray that one day you become kind and respectful of your subjects, especially the old and the weak."

After uttering these words, the old man suddenly disappeared. Everybody was speechless! They were dumbfounded. Rajah Kawayan became weak and sickly after the encounter with the stranger. Not long after, the king died.

Days passed, and a plant grew on the side of his grave, tall and slender like Rajah Kawayan, the evil king that ruled the kingdom many years ago. Those who noticed it say that it always sways and bows its head each time the wind blows. His constituents say that the plant reminds them of Rajah Kawayan, who may have finally learned his lesson of humility and respect for others.

The plant grew taller and taller. Soon enough, it could be found everywhere in the kingdom. The people decided to call it "Kawayan" or bamboo in English as it reminded them of their cruel king.

Introduction

Sometime in 1962, Rogelio Sikat wrote about a native whose classmates teased him every day for having dark skin, a flat nose, and thick lips. He kept cool on many occasions, heeding the advice of his parents not to quarrel with anyone in school. Until he felt he had enough and floored the bigger guy with a punch on his face.

This story happened many times in the past and is still happening today, many decades after, not only in the Philippines but elsewhere in the world. A recent report of ABS-CBN said that at least 6 out of 10 Filipinos are being bullied regularly, while the prevalence of bullying in Philippine schools is nearly three times higher compared to developed countries.

I was born with a physical defect. Instead of five, I have six toes on my left foot. Three of them are joined together. In grade school, I was called 'Ebeng Dikit,' or the girl with ginger toes. I was constantly teased and bullied by kids my age. My generation and the ones before us went to school barefooted, so it was hard for them to miss my physical flaw.

I survived their hurtful jokes, their snickering remarks, their hidden chuckles each time I pass by them or when they see me flip-flopping on the dusty road. I did not let them quash my spirit. I did not let them get on my nerves. I studied hard and remained humble until I graduated at the top of my class that year.

But not every child can muster the courage to face the challenge. Many of them are traumatized and let their emotions cave in. I was lucky to have had parents who kept assuring me that I am loved and that I am as loveable as any human being. Other children do not find the same support from their parents.

Bullying involves two people -- a bully or intimidator and a victim. The bully abuses the victim through physical, verbal, or other means in order to gain a sense of superiority and power. Many children succumb to bullying until they cannot take it anymore, just like Impeng. But they need the support of their parents, their teachers, and their adult community.

Just like me, when I was a child, they needed the assurance that they are loved and they are equal to any other living human.

Dedicated with love to
Paul and Pauline and all
the children of Sumacab,
Cabanatuan City,
Philippines

GINGER TOES TO THE RESCUE

Kablam! The car door closed with a slam. Grandma saw her young granddaughter slumping into the back seat with a doleful face from the rear-view mirror.

"What's the matter, darling?" Grandma had been picking her up after school. But this was the first time Jolie had shown displeasure.

"What happened in school today?" Grandma asked again. "I don't want to talk about it!" Jolie snapped, her lips quivering, her eyes starting to tear up. "It's all right, darling. You don't have to tell me anything now.

"Let's go home," Grandma said and drove away from the curb after checking that Jolie's seat belt was securely fastened.

Often in the past, the little girl couldn't stop talking about her day as soon as she got inside the car. This time she was quiet and seemed very tired.

"We're home. Are you okay, darling?" Grandma asked. Jolie didn't utter a word as she got out of the car. She dashed thru the house as soon as Grandma opened the door. Grandma held back from saying anything else to her.

"Let's not go to the park today, Grandma. I am tired. I just want to rest," Jolie finally spoke as she opened the door.

She and Grandma loved going to the park after school. Especially on such a nice day. They would fill the picnic basket with fruits, crackers and cheese, and fruit drinks and have picnics by the pond.

After the snacks, they would skip pebbles on the water. They would keep score of which stones had traveled the farthest and made the highest leap, using their fingers like a football referee.

"Did you want a snack before you take your nap?"
Grandma asked as she followed and picked up after her.

"No, Grandma, just leave me alone,
please," the little girl pleaded.

Grandma put her hand on top of her granddaughter's
forehead. "Not hot, no fever, I suppose. Perhaps you are just
tired." Grandma closed the door behind her to let the girl
nap.

Tok! Tok! Tok!

Grandma and Jolie heard a key turning in the lock of the front door.

"Mom's home! Where's my Bum-bum?"

Jolie heard her mother's cheerful voice. She got up from her bed and ran down the hallway with a smile on her face. Grandma came from the dining room, where she sat reading a magazine.

Both rushed to the doorway to greet Jane, Jolie's mother.

"Oh, Mom!" Jolie said aloud, hugging her mother. "I'm so glad you're home."

Mom held her daughter in a tight embrace. "Is something the matter, Bum-bum?"

"Nothing," said Jolie, avoiding her mother's glance. Yet, the crack in her voice gave away the hurt she was hiding.

Jane looked at Grandma. In a hushed tone, she asked. "What happened, Grandma?"

Grandma shook her head. "I've asked her about it, but she'd been shutting me out."

"I'm home, too!" Dad John came in from the garage. He went straight to Jolie, picked her up, and stood her on a pink stool by the wall next to the door.

He kissed his daughter on her forehead. "Yuck," Jolie would always jokingly say when Dad kissed her. But this time, her "Yuck!" did not sound cheerful. Jolie's behavior surprised her father.

"What's wrong, Pumpkin?"

John asked. Jolie looked up at Dad, Mom, and Grandma and then looked down. "I said I don't want to talk about it," she said softly and ran back to her room. Dad, Mom, and Grandma exchanged worried looks.

"Maybe dinner will cheer her up," said Grandma. She went to the kitchen to check the food cooking in the oven.

Dad and Mom went to their bedroom to change.

Jolie sat down quietly at the dining table. She ate fast, hardly chewing her food at all.

"Bum-bum, take it easy. Be careful not to choke on the chicken bones," Jane reminded her cheerily.

But Jolie wasn't paying attention to her mother. After swallowing the last bite, she zoomed back to her room like a witch on its broom!

"Something must have happened in school," said Mom.

Dad and Grandma nodded, looking as concerned as Mom.

"I'll see her to bed," offered Grandma.

"Okay, darling, we've got to talk," Grandma told her granddaughter, sitting in a corner in her room.

"I can't, Grandma. I'm angry and hurt," said Jolie.

"Your face will mold into a frown if you keep that up," Grandma said, smiling sweetly at her granddaughter.

The little girl tried to choke her laughter.

"Grandma, do you think I am fat and ugly?" she asked, her brows puckered.

A puzzled Grandma asked, "What made you ask a question like that?"

"Some girls in my school call me fat with big bones," Jolie was nervous as she intertwined her fingers.

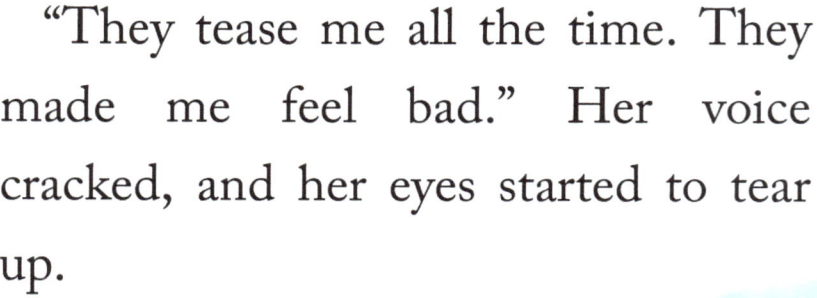

"They tease me all the time. They made me feel bad." Her voice cracked, and her eyes started to tear up.

"I am so sorry, darling," Grandma said, giving her granddaughter a tight embrace. "I don't know what made those bullies say those hurtful words."

11

"Look yourself in the mirror." Grandma pointed the self-standing mirror at a corner of the room.

"Tell me, do you like what you see?"

"Uhmmm, I like my long black shiny hair. My face, I guess, is very fair." The girl began saying as she looked at herself in the mirror. "But to most kids in my class, I am heavier and taller."

"That's why you swim well, darling," said Grandma, smiling at her granddaughter.

"Big arms and broad shoulders, they keep you afloat."

Despite the tears, Jolie smiled.

"Those kids that taunt you," Grandma continued, "are they good in any sports?"

Jolie thought for a second and answered, "I don't know, I don't think so."

"See, darling? There you go," Grandma said, smiling.

The little girl heaved a sigh, now feeling like a heavy burden had been lifted off her chest.

Her lips widened into a smile. "I guess I'm not fat. I just have an athlete's body."

"I'll let you in on a secret. You know, I was teased a lot too when I was about your age," Grandma revealed with an understanding smile.

"Really, Grandma? How come?" Jolie got very curious. She moved closer to her grandmother.

"I was called a freak because my left foot was different from everyone else's," Grandma sighed.

"Oh, they laughed at those?" Jolie said, pointing to her grandmother's left foot where three of its toes were linked together that they looked like a piece of ginger roots.

"Yes, they called me ginger toes," said Grandma, looking sad, as if she was going back to that time in her childhood.

"Poor Grandma," She got closer and gave her grandmother a hug.

"Why do you have ginger toes, Grandma?" Jolie asked.

"My mother said she ate much ginger when I was growing in her tummy," Grandma said.

"Really, Grandma?" Jolie held her laugh and sat steadily, eager to hear Grandma's story.

"Kids in my village during my time walked to school barefoot! And so it was hard to miss my ginger toes."

One afternoon, a bunch of kids started teasing me hard. I was so mad I punched one of them. But I missed my first shot. I lost my balance and face down on the ground. They teased me with ginger toes and a ground kisser.

Jolie moved closer to her grandmother and asked in a comforting voice, "Did you tell your parents?"

Grandmother nodded. "My parents told me to fight back."

"A few days passed, and they came after me again. So, I had to defend myself once more."

"And how did that go, Grandma?" Jolie asked, feeling bad for her grandmother.

"I didn't kiss the ground for the second time. I swam in a fish pond instead." She paused to chuckle.

"The sixth graders were digging a fish pond for their science project. It rained hard the night before. So, the pond was filled with water the following morning."

"They literally forced me into the pond after I came up to them." Grandma tried to catch her breath after finishing her story.

"That's frustrating!" Jolie said, now laughing again with her grandmother.

"Whew!" Grandma exclaimed, trying to catch her breath after laughing hard and long. "I avoided them after that."

"You did?" Jolie said in between laughing and gasping for breath.

"Yes." Grandma had turned serious. "Instead of thinking about how I could get even, I turned my frustrations into studying hard. I got good grades, and the pay-off was sweet."

Jolie's brows knitted. "I don't understand, Grandma."

"Because of my good grades, I became my teacher's assistant," Grandma beamed as she remembered this. "Everyone was now my friend— even those horrible classmates of mine."

"You got back at them, Grandma," said Jolie, nodding her head in agreement.

"And in a very positive way," added Grandma. Jolie kissed her grandmother. "Thank you for telling me your story. I feel so much better now."

"I am glad you do," said Grandma. "Now, get up and talk to your parents. They are worried sick about you."

Tok! Tok! Tok!

"Mom, Dad, can I please come in? I need to talk to you."

"Yes, Bumbum, come in. We want to talk to you, too!" Jane's voice came through the door.

"I don't want to go to school anymore. I just want to stay home with Grandma," Jolie blurted out as soon as she entered the door. Jolie's parents were prepared for this. They sat their daughter on the bed between them two and explained.

"Well, Bumbum, I am afraid that's not possible. You need to go to school so you can learn how to read and write and many other things." Explained Jane.

"Didn't you always say you want to be like your teacher when you grow up?" John tried to sweet-talk her daughter.

"Yes, but maybe Grandma can teach me at home?" Jolie insisted.

"Grandma could teach you some, but not everything. School is the best place for a growing child like you to learn. Now tell us why you don't want to go to school anymore." Both parents were now worried about the direction Jolie's mind was going.

"Two girls in my class are always mean to me. This morning during recess, Eliza pulled my ponytail, and Sandra called me fat. It hurts Mom." Jolie started sobbing.

"Did you tell your teacher," asked Dad. "I just walked away and ignored them. I was afraid they would tease me more and call me a cry baby." Jolie started sobbing.

"You did great, Bumbum." Her mother nodded.

"But what about tomorrow? I am afraid they will do that to me again!" "Okay, let's talk more about this." Mom and Dad suggested.

"What should I do when they start teasing me again?" The now calmed little girl asked.

"Stand up for yourself," Mom said, "but continue to keep your distance."

"That sounds easy but hard to do," Jolie told her mother. "What if they keep repeating it?"

"Then it's to me to speak out. Don't hesitate to tell your teacher or someone else you trust," her father stated.

"It is the teacher's job and the school's responsibility to make you feel safe," Jolie's father said. "If they refuse to help you, let us know right away. We will talk to them."

"Or I'll do what Grandma did when she was bullied in school!" Jolie started to lighten up.

Her parents became curious. "Oh yeah?" asked Mom. "What did she do?"

Jolie told them the story of how Grandma dealt with the bullies in her school. "She focused on getting good grades. As for me, I will concentrate on my swimming."

Mom and Dad smiled admiringly at their little girl. "That sounds like a good way to deal with bullies, Pumpkin!" her father agreed.

Grandma fetched a peppy little girl from school the following day.

"How was school today, darling?" Grandma asked her as soon as she had buckled up.

"Fine, Grandma. I played with Eliza and Sandra during recess. They didn't tease me, but I would not be afraid when they do. Mom and Dad had told me what to do," the cheerful girl said with confidence.

"That's my darling." Grandma's smile was sweeter than pie.

"Oh, Grandma, can we stop at the flower shop before we go home?"

"Hmmm …flowers for Mom?"

"It's a secret," Jolie answered teasingly.

Grandma started the car engine. Tsskterr, vrroommm!

It revved to life as if it had awakened from a trance.

At the dining table that night, Jolie handed a bouquet of flowers each to her mother and grandmother.

"Mom, Grandma, Thank you for being here for me. I love you both."

"And what about your poor old dad?" John jokingly said.

A happy girl ran to her father, gave him a hug, and kissed him on one cheek. "I love you, too, Daddy!"

Grandma, Mom, and Dad beamed at the happy girl! "Now, let's go eat before the food gets cold," said Dad. "I am so hungry I could eat a horse."

Everybody laughed at Dad's words.

Nieves Catahan Villamin – writer of nonfiction, history enthusiast, and social advocate.

Her first book Bittermelons and Mimosas: A Philippine Memoir, gives a fascinating look at a life short on luxuries but long in compassion, joy, and family that will inspire other Filipinos who strive for a piece of the American Dream.

An indispensable reference for anyone interested in Philippine history, customs, and superstitions, Cal Poly San Luis Obispo SLO Ethnic Department students used the book as required reading material in the winter and spring of 2012. *Taguan with Eden and Friends, One Moonlit Night with Magical Creatures, A Summer Feast, and S.O.S., Sink or Swim Ginger Toes* are the children's books she wrote and were adaptations from her memoir.

Paul Lucero - illustrator and graphic designer

He's a Senior High School student in the Emirates. He lives with his loving and supportive parents, Rhea Lynn Lucero and Rolando Lucero, and his sister, Pauline Lucero. He likes to excel in different types of extracurricular activities. He is currently pursuing school as he has many big dreams he wishes to accomplish. He is a young man who likes to exceed above and beyond.

Pauline Lucero - illustrator

She's a young artist in the Emirates. She is an elementary student that lives with her loving and supportive parents, Rhea Lynn Lucero and Rolando Lucero, and her brother Paul Lucero. She has this unexplainable passion for art. At present, she is getting ready to transition to high school.